The Powerful Pulley

Julie Murray

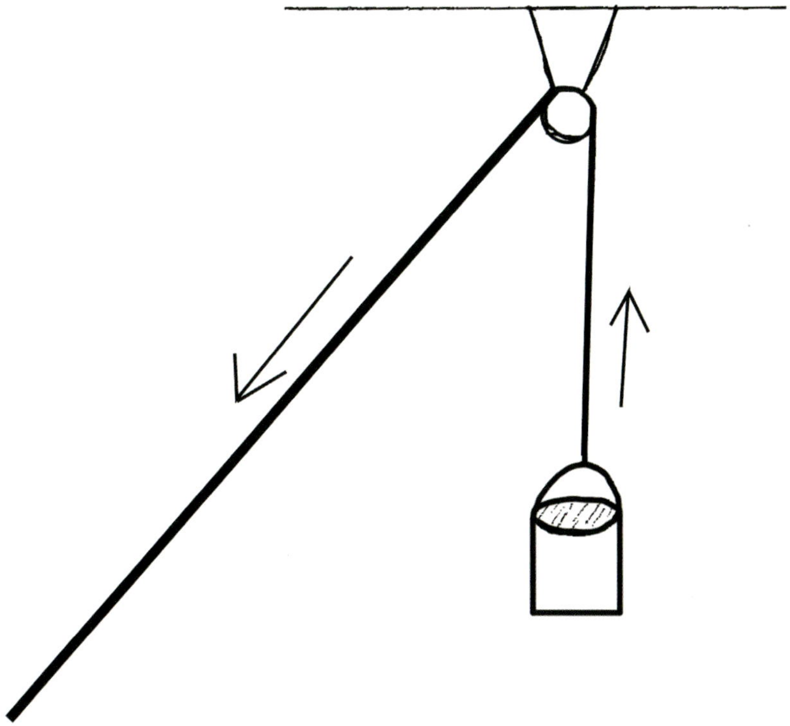

Abdo Kids Junior
is an Imprint of Abdo Kids
abdobooks.com

Abdo Kids
SIMPLE MACHINES

abdobooks.com

Published by Abdo Kids, a division of ABDO, P.O. Box 398166, Minneapolis, Minnesota 55439.

Printed in the United States of America, North Mankato, Minnesota.

052024

092024

THIS BOOK CONTAINS RECYCLED MATERIALS

Photo Credits: Getty Images, Shutterstock

Production Contributors: Teddy Borth, Jennie Forsberg, Grace Hansen

Design Contributors: Candice Keimig, Pakou Moua

Library of Congress Control Number: 2023948559

Publisher's Cataloging-in-Publication Data

Names: Murray, Julie, author.

Title: The powerful pulley / by Julie Murray

Description: Minneapolis, Minnesota : Abdo Kids, 2025 | Series: Simple machines | Includes online resources and index.

Identifiers: ISBN 9798384900610 (lib. bdg.) | ISBN 9798384901310 (ebook) | ISBN 9798384901662 (Read-to-me eBook)

Subjects: LCSH: Simple machines--Juvenile literature. | Pulleys--Juvenile literature. | Hoisting machinery--Juvenile literature. | Machinery--Juvenile literature. | Hand tools--Juvenile literature.

Classification: DDC 621.8--dc23

Table of Contents

The Powerful Pulley

A pulley is a simple machine.

It is used to move a **load**.

53
54
4
86

The parts of a pulley work together.

A pulley has a wheel and axle. A line sits in the wheel's **groove**.

wheel
axle
line
groove

The line connects to the **load**.

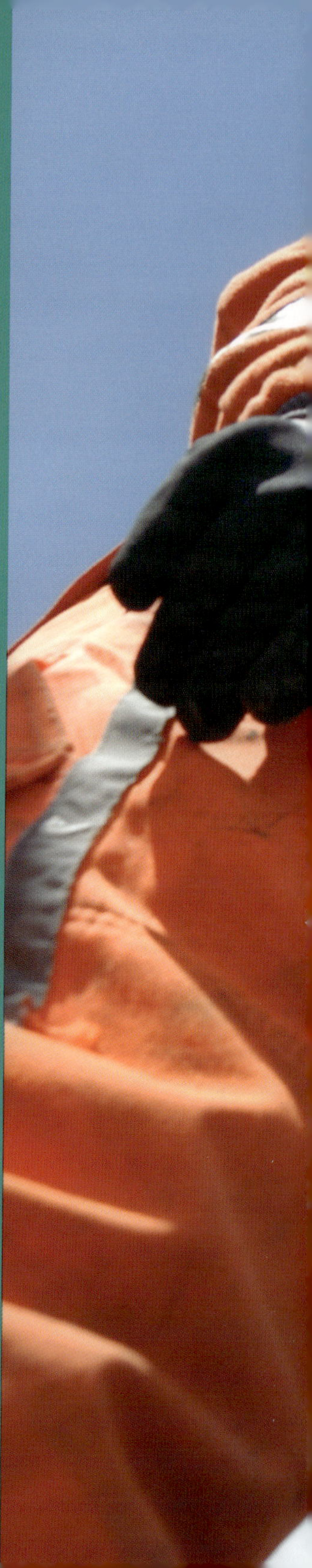

line
load

The **load** needs to be moved.

The wheel rotates on its axle when the line is pulled.

line
wheel
and axle
load

Force is used to pull the line. This moves the **load**.

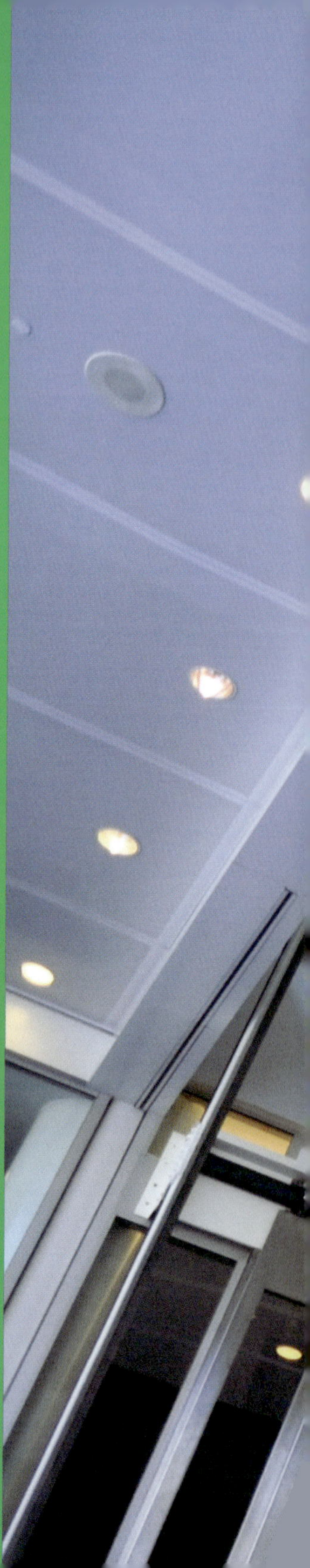

A pulley makes moving a **load** easier!

Pulleys Around You

crane

elevator

fishing reel

flagpole

Glossary

force

power, energy, or physical strength.

groove

a long, narrow cut in a surface.

load

an amount of something carried.

Index